# *The*
# PARISH GUIDE
# TO SOCIAL MEDIA

How social networking can *recharge* your ministry

## Clarissa Valbuena Aljentera

TWENTY
THIRD *2317*
PUBLICATIONS
NEW LONDON, CT 06320
WWW.23RDPUBLICATIONS.COM

*For Dad, Mom, and Lawrence:*
*Your laughter, compassion, and*
*encouragement helped me to fly.*
*I love you for all of it and more.*

TWENTY-THIRD PUBLICATIONS

A Division of Bayard

One Montauk Avenue, Suite 200

New London, CT 06320

(860) 437-3012 or (800) 321-0411

www.23rdpublications.com

ISBN: 978-1-58595-902-0

Library of Congress Control Number: 2013932073

Printed in the U.S.A.

# Contents

# Being Present and Accountable in a Busy World

**STANDING IN THE SHARED KITCHEN AT WORK DURING LUNCHTIME,** I often catch snippets of what people did on their weekend or whose daughter is home sick from daycare. As we shuffle about taking turns sharing stories and scooting around each other to get into the refrigerator and over to the sink, we share our lives in an informal way with those around us. Our encounters are brief yet meaningful, because we will return to that same spot and update each other on the daughter who is on the mend and on our plans for this weekend's adventures.

Social media works in much the same way. It is an immediate and real-time way of sharing our lives with each other. Like a workplace kitchen, social media is a place to gather and communicate. It is also a place where people are fed.

Social media can be used to expand our ministries, as this book will show. Social networking at its core is a place of welcome for our parishioners. In the following chapters we will explore ways to move into social networks in order to integrate them into specific ministries. Many parishes have already harnessed the promotional aspect of social media. Here we'll look at ways to develop a more complete picture of how your parish can benefit from it. Understanding and using different forms of social media, both separately and in conjunction with others, is a vibrant way to share the gospel message.

Chapters 1 and 2 offer an overview of social media and a primer on some of the most popular sites. Chapters 3 and 4 provide ideas for putting social networking into place for specific ministries. Chapter 5 contains some cautionary advice about the pitfalls inherent in social media as well as its potential for recharging our ministries and enlivening our call to spread the gospel. At the back of the book are two charts: one listing organizations with guidelines for ensuring a safe and appropriate use of this technology, and one summarizing the key features of various social media sites.

Much like a kitchen is more than just a room to house appliances and prepare food, social networks have greater potential beyond storing photographs and sharing tidbits of news. Applied to pastoral ministry, social media is an exciting way to connect with those within our parishes and beyond them in order to further the work of the church.

# CHAPTER 1

# What Makes Social Media Important for Parish Ministry?

*A 33-YEAR-OLD MOTHER OF TWO DAUGHTERS EN-JOYS CATCHING UP ON SOCIAL MEDIA TO SEE PHOTOS AND STORIES OF HER FRIENDS AND THEIR FAMILIES. She and her husband have a four-year-old and a one-year-old whose photos are often posted online. She is drawn into Facebook and uses it as a place to keep and share memories and stories of her two girls.*

The woman I've just described probably sounds like a member of your parish. Certainly there are many people like her in all our parishes, and social networking is increasingly important in their lives. Think of just some of the ways this networking is impacting our world:

## Six ways social media is changing our lives

■ *Social media helps us reach out to others in new ways.* A mother who uses social media to share news about her daughter's soccer team is telling the world how proud she is of her child's accomplishments. Someone else might use networking sites to display photos of their house that is currently up for sale. An organization can use social media as a tool to share information and photos of activities and events.

■ *Today's social media sites allow us to share news with each other on our own terms.* We log into social networking sites and talk about our weekend activities, the weather forecast, or news updates. Instead of standing around chatting with two other people, social networking allows us to broaden conversations to include dozens of people. Some are interested listeners while others are active talkers. Some just pass through without much interaction other than a glance.

■ *Social media helps close the distance between us.* Former co-workers can keep up with one another by sharing information and photographs. Grandparents connect with their grandchildren between visits. We might reconnect and recharge relationships that started in high school or college or after the birth of a child. Instead of losing ongoing contact with people we care about, social media allows us to keep up.

■ *Social media sites allow the freedom to explore and the inspiration to find something new.* Connections can be made to new ministries and new friends. Our creativity can be harnessed through photographs and words and shared with others. Relationship building is a constant with social media. These sites are used for individuals as well as for groups and organizations.

■ *Social networks have changed how we view communication.* We expect to be part of the conversation instead of simply listening or receiving information. Organizations invite us to post comments, thus encouraging dialog with a broader audience. We are asked for our thoughts and opinions and then offered a venue for sharing them immediately.

■ *With social networks, communication through media is no longer one-sided.* In the past, people who watched television and listened to the radio were not able to interact with each other. Technology has made it possible for people to respond in immediate fashion to something they read, watch, or listen to. In doing so, they become part of the conversation. Through our responses, others get a sense of who we are and what we believe. They begin to understand what is important to us.

**What does social networking have to do with my parish?**
Used well, it can bring great benefits to your parish.

*First, it builds connections and relationships.* Think of parishioners with an active faith life. How and where do they connect with the parish? They might attend Sunday Mass or volunteer for parish ministries and projects. Some might also be daily Mass goers or catechists. These people find life-giving ways to live their faith.

These kinds of faith connections and activities are crucial to the life of your parish and its people, and social media is not a substitute for any of them. But what social media can do is help enhance those faith connections and help to bring more and more people into life-giving relationships within your parish. Relationships are at the heart of our faith. Through relationships with others, we can express and receive God's love in both communal and personal ways. Online connections allow a wider range of contact and relationships—and the prospects for a parish can be exciting.

*Second, it promotes evangelization and outreach.* Social media can also be the welcoming, faith-filled "face" your parish presents to the world. It can be the place where people "meet" your parish for the first time. Someone might initially attend an event or find out information about a particular ministry through a social network. This connection might, in turn, evolve through other online features, such as the ability to sign a parish guestbook or listen to a podcast of a recent Sunday sermon.

Establishing a welcoming environment through social media might also entail the use of photographs and graphics. These small pieces attract visitors to a site either because they recognize someone they know or see themselves involved in a meaningful way. Using candid photos along with ones that are more formal lightens the atmosphere and showcases a parish's warmth and sense of fun. Unlike pictures that appear in a directory or hang in the parish hall, those on social media sites capture life as it happens. They show a side that is real and full of life.

The success of social networking hinges on its consistent use, something that will be covered in more detail in succeeding chapters of this book. Unlike purchasing new signage for the front of a parish, something that is usually done once, establishing a social media presence is very much like posting a welcome each and every Sunday. The doors are opened in anticipation of new and old friends alike.

*Third, it brings new energy to parish activities.* Social networking can also be used to rally enthusiasm and excitement around annual activities that may have lost their steam. It can create and reinforce community building for religious education classes, youth activities, and other parish programs. The community at large can learn about and track parish social justice activities, thereby using social media as a vehicle for evangelization and witness.

*Fourth, it extends parish life past the physical boundaries and schedules.* Through the use of social networking, the activity in a parish on Sunday mornings can continue through virtual interaction during the week. It is a cycle where one action feeds into another. A confirmation preparation program for adolescents, for example, can include a component in which the confirmandi share their experiences with those who are preparing for next year's class. In such a way, online activity allows conversations to take place beyond our physical doors. Good news spreads in new and engaging ways.

## Our parishioners are way ahead of us!

Statistics released in 2012 by the Center for Applied Research in the Apostolate (CARA) at Georgetown University showed 62 percent of U.S. adult Catholics have a profile on Facebook, and more than 50 percent of Catholics under the age of 30 share photographs and content at least once a week through a social media site. This same group shares something on a social media site daily; of those under 70, about 43 percent visit YouTube to watch videos. These statistics show the breadth of social networking and how it is used. It also makes a strong case for learning more about and expanding ways to use this powerful tool in our parishes

Slowly, those who staff or volunteer for the church in some capacity are making the decision to maintain a virtual presence, whether on their own or within their ministries. Together we are coming to understand that, in order to function and have a relevant voice among the faithful today, we need to become part of this online conversation.

How we function together as a ministry or as a parish reflects how we are sharing God's love with each other. Within our individual ministries, there are distinct ways of using social media to connect and share with those we serve. For those who work with liturgical ministry, for example, social media can offer ways to provide resources for eucharistic ministers, lectors, altar servers, music ministries, and greeters—helping them to find daily inspiration or prepare for Sunday Mass on their own. In youth ministry, social media sites can be used to help fundraise for a service trip. Pastoral council members could use it to upload documents and photos in between meetings.

## NEXT...

▶ Practicality and simplicity are two things to consider when looking at avenues to use social media in ministry. The ideas mentioned above are just a few ways social media can be used in a parish setting. This makes it an extension of who we are and what we believe. Before embarking on the applications for social media in a parish setting, however, let's first make sure we understand some of the basic sites and how they are used.

## THOUGHTS TO PONDER...

- *Are there people in your life who are active users of social media? What do they use social media sites for? Keeping in touch? Networking? Posting news?*

- *What makes you hesitant about using social media for your parish or ministry?*

- *What possibilities for social media do you see in your parish or ministry?*

# Pope Benedict XVI set up a Twitter account— do you have one?

Many leaders in the Catholic Church are embracing social media and using it in their own way to preach the gospel to people around the world. Among them is Pope Benedict XVI, who officially joined Twitter in December of 2012 with the user name Pontifex. In its first week, his Twitterfeed picked up more than half a million followers. His first "tweet" – a message containing 140 characters or less – read: "Dear friends, I am pleased to get in touch with you through Twitter. Thank you for your generous response. I bless all of you from my heart."

In his address for the 45th World Communications Day, Pope Benedict urged Christians to seriously think about entering the digital age. In his message he stressed the importance of being a good witness to the gospel not just in our face-to-face interactions, but also through technology. The pope talked about new doors that could be opened with social media and how we need to reflect on our relationships with technology. He also noted that social media is not simply an excuse to insert expressly religious content onto different social media sites. It is a way to use modern technology to witness to the gospel message in meaningful and widespread ways.

There are other examples of Catholic leaders and organizations that are making the foray into social media. In the archdioceses of Boston and Chicago, Cardinals Sean O'Malley and Francis George, respectively, use social media as a platform to inform parishioners about the issues in the local news. One example was tweeting messages to help defeat a ballot initiative on assisted suicide. Another was creating a short video on YouTube explaining religious freedom. Sr. Helen Prejean, a sister with the Congregation of St. Joseph, uses social media to speak out against the death penalty. And, of course, Catholic publishers are using social media to publicize resources, publish blogs, and broadcast webinars.

# CHAPTER 2

# Familiarizing Yourself with Social Media: A Social Media Primer

**SEVERAL SOCIAL MEDIA SITES HOLD POTENTIAL FOR USE WITHIN PARISH MINISTRY.** Each one has its upsides and downsides, but they are all relatively easy to learn. Let's look at distinct characteristics of some of these networks and how each site runs. (See pages 65-72 for a table containing a brief summary of the features of each of these sites.)

Here is the Facebook page for Zeb's House at St. James. We displayed a picture of our church, and our profile photo is a group photo. You have a sense of who is involved in the ministry and can learn a little more about our ministry.

**Facebook** – a site originally constructed with college students in mind. Its inventors were aware of what its users wanted to learn from their classmates and friends. The site is now enormously popular across intergenerational lines and boasts more than nine hundred million active users. Facebook is the site many people use to jump into social media.

Features on Facebook include photo posting, news sharing, staying in touch with former classmates and old friends, and playing games online with friends. It has become a catchall for users who log on to find out information and learn more about each other. Having a Facebook page is the equivalent of having a functional and current website.

Facebook has also become a primary network for business and professional purposes. Many businesses and organizations set up a fan page. By "liking" a page individuals can show their support for something, and businesses get a boost in visibility and favorability. These specific pages can help increase an organization or individual's presence and encourage involvement from other users who also became fans.

Parishes can create a single Facebook page or several that focus on various ministries. Parishes can use Facebook to post links to Sunday readings or parish videos, or they can create a closed online group for faith sharing. The latter restricts participation and offers another way for parishioners to participate in a program from their home or while traveling.

**Twitter** – a site that offers a quick and easy way to share short, succinct pieces of news and information. Twitter users send and receive "tweets," which are 140-character (or less) messages, thoughts, or ideas. Users have the option of making their Twitter profiles public or private. This means a user can open up their profile to a wide audience or limit it to a small group of readers. Many people use Twitter in conjunction with another site or post their tweets on a web page for updated and instant news and reminders. Organizations primarily use the site for sharing news updates and photographs in a timely manner. In some cases, Twitter users remind each other of events or outings. Users can advertise events on this site.

Because it is also accessible through smart phones, news can be sent and received in instantaneous fashion. Twitter might help parishes best when it comes to making short and timely announcements related to church-related events. It can also be used in conjunction with a parish web page, to broadcast up-to-date information, or to provide references to Sunday readings.

Here are a handful of Twitter profiles on one page that depict several items. There are several Twitter users who are using Twitter for various uses: personal, professional, and news sharing. Each of the displayed Twitter profiles has a different audience.

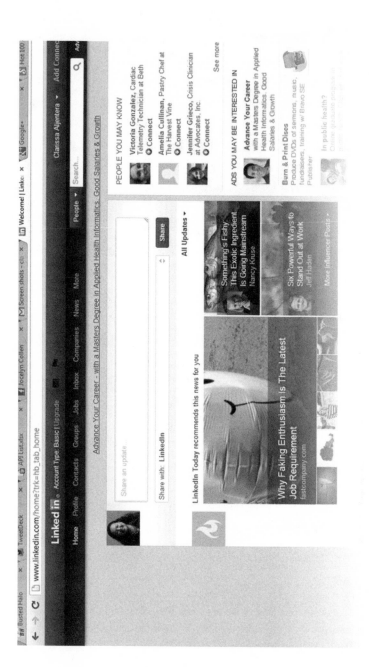

**in** **LinkedIn** – a site primarily used for business or work-related connections. LinkedIn allows users to create individual profiles as a way to keep in touch with colleagues or business associates. In addition to allowing users to share business and work-related information, LinkedIn is a place to connect with potential employees and employers. Some use it to keep in touch with professional organizations or alumni groups. Recent college graduates and young professionals turn to this site to generate and maintain contacts in seeking referrals and endorsements. LinkedIn users can create specific groups as a way to remain connected professionally. Within these groups you can post specific discussion content, such as articles, or ask the group a question for all to answer. These functions give users another way to engage in a meaningful way.

Parishes can use LinkedIn to create special groups for parishioners as a means of sharing resources. In this way, it can provide information for parishioners who are in the midst of a job search or seeking professional services provided by other parishioners. LinkedIn groups are a creative way to generate discussion as a follow-up to adult religious education programs or to begin online book clubs.

This LinkedIn page allows users to share updates and news. Users will always notice important news that LinkedIn recommends for individual users.

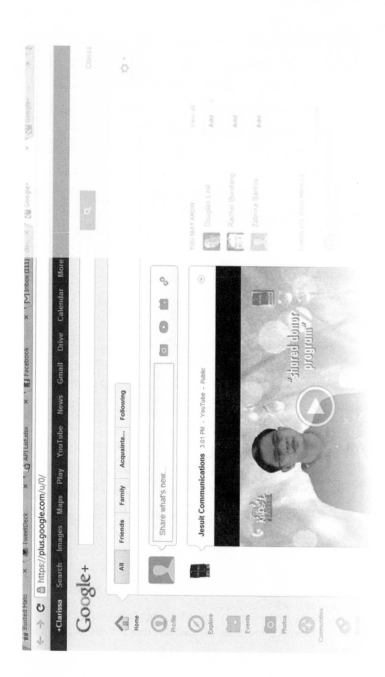

**Google+** – a site that allows people to specifically target a social media audience. Information and photos can be shared with different people at various levels, much like pulling together a circle of friends from high school and from former jobs. This site provides opportunities for networking through video chats and conferencing. It also allows users to post videos, thus making it a multimedia hub. There is great potential for creating a learning environment that lends itself to collaboration.

Parish leaders might use Google+ to share liturgical schedules and meeting agendas more easily. It also has the capability for video conferencing as a way to hold online planning or evaluation meetings.

Google+ organizes connections and has a layout on its page that makes it easier to find information. This personal Google+ account is connected with organizations that use social media to share information.

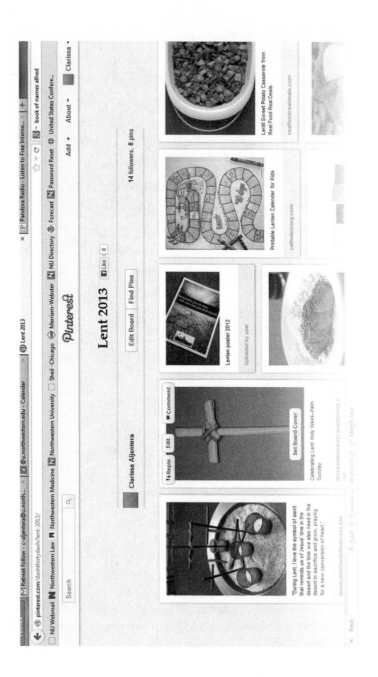

**Pinterest** – a site that sorts items digitally, much like posting them on a corkboard in a kitchen. Users "pin" items to specific boards to keep track of things and generate themes. Pinning is the equivalent of copying and saving a web link to a specific page. Users can save images to specific boards that can then be categorized and shared publicly with others.

Pinterest has great potential for religious education classes as a way to showcase children's projects. Liturgical ministers might also consider creating boards for Advent and Lent as a way to draw parishioners in through photos and words in a thematic way.

This Pinterest board was created with a lenten theme that organizes lenten projects, images, and recipes that will help through the liturgical season. Users can share pictures and resources easily.

Busted Halo

**Description**

Busted Halo is network of media and ministry for young adult spiritual seekers that creates a responsive and engaging community where people can discuss the intersection of faith, culture, politics, and life.

**Links**

Submit your questions of faith here!
bustedhalo.com
facebook.com/bustedhalo
twitter.com/bustedhalo

— TEXT —
#busted halo
#MicroChallenge
#book
#read

**MicroChallenge - February 3**

Today, start a book that you have been meaning to read for a while.

— PHOTO —
#busted halo
#Daily pic
#read
#book
#death
#aj o'rourke
#sprint

Always read something that will make you look good if you die in the middle of it.
—P.J. O'Rourke

— INFO —
2 days ago
Reblog

— TEXT —
#busted halo
#MicroChallenge
#love

**MicroChallenge - February 2**

Make an unprompted gesture of love for someone dear to you today.

— PHOTO —
#busted halo
#Daily pic
#San Francisn
#love

— INFO —
2 notes
2 days ago
Reblog

— INFO —
3 days ago
Reblog

**t** **Tumblr** – a site that allows users to share videos, quotes, links, photographs, and ideas. It is instant publishing that offers a variety of options and can be done on the go with a smart phone or from your computer. This site has the potential to hold many pieces of multimedia in one place for an easy-to-find reference. Tumblr is considered a better platform for blogging than most other sites. When blogs first became popular, users needed to share photos and re-post other blogger's items on their own sites. Tumblr now gives someone the ability to re-post and load photographs all in one place with little effort.

Youth ministers might use Tumblr to post various photos of events and activities in a manner similar to Pinterest. Because it is a catchall site, there is also the potential to use it to post videos and create blogs.

This Tumblr profile belongs to Busted Halo, a ministry created by the Paulist Fathers that is aimed at people in their twenties and thirties. This Tumblr shares daily challenges that are meant to have users think about how to encounter God in small ways.

**YouTube** – a site that allows users to share and distribute video and video clips. Videos on this site range from those produced by professional musicians and filmmakers with enormous followings to those of amateurs who are looking for an online audience. Many use this site to capture and share original content. It has a particular appeal for those who want to use videos as a storytelling method.

YouTube users can create specific channels for their viewers if they are creating multiple videos. This enables those accessing the site to have a home base as a way to look for material and maintain a digital video library. Parishes could use the site to do the latter as well as to create and share parish videos with a larger audience.

**Flickr or Picasa** – sites for sharing photographs without charge. In addition to sharing pictures, users can create storage for photographs of weddings, family reunions, and other events. Groups can set up accounts to share event photos from previous years.

Parishes might use these sites as a way to share photos of parish renovation projects, social events, or special Masses. Some parishes create links to their Flickr or Picasa sites on their websites. This provides parishioners access to a photo library of parish history.

**Podcasts** – Podcasts are audio recordings that can be downloaded or streamed to a user's computer. (The difference between a download and a stream is that the download can be saved and listened to at a later time and a stream is something that the user listens to right away, while connected to the site.) Podcasts are a relatively old medium compared to the social media listed above. Nevertheless, they have a wide range of uses that includes sharing lectures in an academic context, sharing homilies from Sunday Mass, or even recording individually produced shows that can be broadcast worldwide. The appeal of the podcast is that it gives people an opportunity to listen to something that they either missed or want to revisit.

The sites described above all have potential for engaging parishioners, new and old, in an easy way. Since each one is free, cost is not a prohibitive factor in making use of social media. This is a real-time way to share with others around us.

## Putting social media sites to work for your parish

The best way to use social media sites is in the ways they were intended. YouTube is great for videos and multimedia sharing, so make use of it when filming classes or talks. Pinterest is useful for collecting items to share and putting things onto distinct boards for all to see. Consider creating a category for themes of the liturgical year, for example, or inspirational sayings that help people pray their way through the day.

- *Use sites in tandem.* Many social media sites can also be used in conjunction with each other. "Techies" call this multiplatform use. This term simply means that it is no longer necessary to rely on a single means of sharing or publicizing all the good things happening in a ministry or parish. Much like parishes do not rely solely on their Sunday bulletin to share everything that goes on, the same principle applies to social networking. It is not enough to set up a Facebook page or even a website. To be effective, other steps must be taken in order to broaden the number of users in a community. How, then, does multiplatform use work?

Pinterest and YouTube work well together for seasonal programs, such as Lent or Advent, because both lend themselves to generating and keeping themes in one place. They also do a great job of explaining stories in a visual way. In like manner, two types of social media might be used together to explain what children are doing to prepare for first reconciliation. The parish could use Twitter to share specific Scripture verses about forgiveness and to highlight stories in the Bible related to reconciliation. Say, for example, the children did an art and crafts project to illustrate that, through reconciliation, we come to experience God's love in a deeper way. Parents can take pictures of the art projects and pin them to a Pinterest board. This involves parents in the preparation for reconciliation and shows other parishioners the formation of their children's faith.

■ *Incorporate social media into your parish website.* In the early days of the internet, the big push was to establish a website so people could easily find basic parish information: physical address, Mass times, wedding information, etc. While websites are still valuable, nothing much changes from week to week. Placing podcasts of sermons or other talks on a parish website makes it a more active environment and encourages parishioners to visit the site more frequently. Providing links on a website to social media sites, such as Pinterest, Facebook, or Tumblr, is easy to do and widens the range of communication possibilities.

■ *Use social media to draw people to your parish website.* Social media can widen its potential by drawing attention to a website as a resource for parishioners. Twitter lets users know when a new podcast or other piece of information is available on a parish website, for example, or a Facebook posting offers a teaser for a parish program and link to the web page for registration and additional information.

■ *Encourage parishioners to use their smart phones.* Using social media does not always mean having to be tied to your computer. Things that were previously updated through computer programs and software can now be changed with the swipe of a screen or the touch of a button. Parish leaders and parishioners can engage in Twitter or Facebook while they are at a fundraiser or social activity by posting live information. For example, snapping a photo at a meet and greet and taking a few moments to post it while the event is happening will help generate instant news. Many organizations that use Twitter will often do a "live tweet," which is the equivalent of a sports announcer giving "play-by-play." That might be helpful in town-hall meetings or larger gatherings where information is shared in a community format.

## NEXT...

▶ Now that we have looked at various kinds of social media and how they can work together, let's move to some ideas for putting it to work in your parish.

## THOUGHTS TO PONDER...

- *Which site or sites would you like to try out for your parish or ministry? What would be a reasonable deadline to set this up? Six months? One month? Two weeks?*

- *Take a look at your parish website. How might social media enhance the use of the website for your parishioners?*

# A firsthand account of how social media can work in a parish

For the past two years, my parish, St. James, on Wabash Avenue in Chicago, has held an Oktoberfest sponsored by Zeb's House, the young adult ministry. The first year, we published the event in the bulletin and made announcements every Sunday. We also advertised the event on Facebook, hoping that greater numbers of people would attend. It was a fun event that drew in mostly young adults and a handful of others who wanted to support our ministry at St. James.

Taking this example, here are some ideas for using various social media to talk about the Oktoberfest and Zeb's House. The first Oktoberfest focused on the theme of gratitude and the abundance that we had received as a parish. One of the young adults created a collage, and another wrote a prayer and opening activity that set the tone that night.

Fast forward one year, when Zeb's House hosts the event again. This time, organizers want to draw greater attention to the theme of gratitude. In order to prepare attendees for the event, they might use Twitter to post one or two Scripture stories around gratitude and thanksgiving. These are tweeted along with a few words about Oktoberfest. Pinterest might also be used to pin pictures of food and recipes that are associated with Oktoberfest.

Those examples can generate awareness around Zeb's House and the Oktoberfest event. They clearly use the specific social networking sites in the ways they were intended: sharing news and passing along images. It also broadens the conversation and provides venues for focusing on the central aspects of the event: Scripture, sharing of a meal, and remembering through photographs.

# CHAPTER 3

# Integrating Social Media into Parish Ministry

**THE LAST CHAPTER OFFERED INFORMATION ABOUT SOCIAL MEDIA AND HOW IT IS USED.** In this chapter, let's look at ways to incorporate social media into parish ministry. The following examples highlight some of the ways this can be done.

**Example 1: Social media and publicizing parish programs**

*St. Cecilia's Parish holds an annual food drive every October. The first few years were very successful but participation has dwindled. Now just a dozen or so families contribute. Publicity*

*for the event is limited to the Sunday bulletin and pulpit an-*
*nouncements.*

Social media could help the people at St. Cecilia's increase participation in their food drive by simply giving
it more exposure. The parish website could be used for
basic information such as time, date, place, and particular items needed for the food drive. Word could then
spread via a parish Facebook page. Many social networking sites offer ways to post an "update," which is an easy
way of saying, "This is new today."

If someone on the planning committee has a Facebook
page, they can start the chain of news by posting a sim-
ple message: "St. Cecilia's is hosting a food drive this
Saturday from 9 AM to 11 AM. Please bring your canned
goods to the parish hall. We are also looking to collect
toothbrushes and toothpaste. Please re-post to spread the
word." That information is then spread from one person
to another with little effort.

In addition to the parish bulletin, website, and
Facebook pages, photos from the previous year's food
drive could be placed on the parish Flickr account. Once
posted, updates can be made through a Flickr account
album. Broaden the involvement by asking liturgical
ministers to advertise the food drive by coming up with
a favorite Scripture story that addresses giving to those
in need. This can be tweeted with a message that might
look something like this: "We learn through the feeding
of the 5,000 that a small amount can go a long way. Share
your bounty with others –MT15. #StCeciliafooddrive"

Text messaging is another means of publicizing events. Many organizations, from airlines to retailers, text news and information. It is often a preferred method of communication for busy people whose cell phones are always within reach. The short reminder is useful for those busy with family responsibilities and work duties.

Once conversation moves beyond the parish through one or more means of social networking, it reaches a much larger pool of people. Once information is circulating online, it is easy to pass it along to others. Peer-to-peer sharing is how social media is best used for parish events and individual ministries.

## Example 2: Raising awareness and participation for a parish program

*San Carlos Cathedral is preparing to restart its youth group after summer break. One goal is to involve a larger number of adolescents and adult volunteers. A small number of young people took part in a service project the year before and became highly engaged with the program as a result. Youth group leaders want to use that experience to generate enthusiasm for another service project, this one out of state, later in the year.*

Since some teenagers have grown a little weary of Facebook, Tumblr provides another means of building excitement around programs and offers a way to share news and information about important events. Tumblr was created as a site for niche bloggers and has appeal for people trying to create a very specific audience. Tumblr also gives a user the ability to upload media in any number of ways—including video, photos, text—and the ability to easily share links.

Here's how this site might work with the Cathedral of San Carlos youth group:

- Those who took part in the previous year's project could share photos of their finished product. If there was a song that best captured their experience, it could be shared on Tumblr, thus combining two forms of media on a single site.

- A video, also posted on Tumblr, would add to the conversation and allow for instant feedback from teens interested in knowing more about the parish program and upcoming project.

- Parents and other adults in the parish can use the Tumblr feed to get updates on fundraising efforts and learn more details about the project.

- After the trip is completed, the site can be used to share photos, media, and blogs about the experience; these serve not only to publicize future events, but also to spread the word about the youths' efforts to the entire parish.

Members of the planning group for the service project could create a group on LinkedIn that could solicit funds from parishioners and their places of business, such as a local restaurant. Members of the parish finance committee might offer ideas through their LinkedIn group regarding fundraising efforts that drew the largest number of donors.

### Example 3: Facilitating collaboration with other parish ministers

*St. Joseph Parish wants to partner with other parishes throughout the diocese to share resources for religious education. They have already started to collaborate with St. Patrick's Parish for an eighth-grade confirmation program. Both parishes have part-time directors of religious education (DREs) and are trying to be creative with resources. Since both are relatively small parishes, it makes sense to combine program resources and their efforts.*

In this example, one DRE has used the same program for years, while the other one has explored materials from a publisher that combines internet resources and textbooks. They can share planning resources via Google+ by using Google drive and participating in a Google Hangout, an online video chat site. A function called Screenshare allows them to share exactly what each is working on in real-time. Instead of e-mailing documents back and forth to develop a common curriculum, Google+ and Google Hangout give the two DREs an ability to work on something together while remaining in their separate locations. Through the use of a web cam with sound capabilities, they can conduct online meetings. They can broaden their conversations in this way with up to 10 people at one time.

Using Google in this way can allow the DREs in this example to share lesson plans and registration sheets, and to build documents together. There is also a way to watch videos together and still be in communication via Google+. To preview media together, they can start the video and pause it while using a chat feature to take notes. Online collaboration helps both DREs feel like they are working together in the same room, as opposed to sending documents and links back and forth. The geographical distance between both parishes automatically becomes smaller.

Social networking creates virtual communities and facilitates a more accessible means of mutual support. It is also helpful for sharing resources, and for bringing people together to brainstorm and create dialog.

**Example 4: Facilitating collaboration between parishes**

*St. Rose and St. Therese parishes have been participating in prison ministry for several years. They are looking for ways to put their volunteers in touch with each other even though they are miles apart from one another. Once or twice a month, volunteers from different parishes take turns to visit the prison.*

Participating in prison ministry is a rich experience for those involved, and it thus lends itself to a great deal of reflection. Facebook can be a tool to facilitate this. A user can create a closed group in which only members have access to the shared information. Leaders within the group can create a space for people to share reflections from their week or even try and incorporate the Sunday gospel into their ministry. For example, each person in the group can be responsible for providing a reflection a few times during the year. A person might write about what a ministry brought to their life. Leaders can encourage members to use each other as resources and to use the site as a way to introduce the ministry to newcomers.

These are just a few examples of the many possibilities for using social media in ministry. They illustrate how social networking can be used for communication, publicity, collaboration, reflection, building community, and offering mutual support. The latter is especially important in order to sustain various ministries and those who devote time to them.

**NEXT...**

▶ In the next chapter, we will look at how to get others on board with social media so that it becomes a parish-wide effort.

**THOUGHTS TO PONDER...**

- *How might you collaborate with other ministers by using social media? How can you start the conversation with them?*

- *How might you engage teenagers via social networking?*

- *Think about one ministry where you might collaborate with a colleague in another parish? How might you get started?*

- *What is one parish project that could use revision? Or could be refreshed?*

# Getting teens involved through social media

Adults working or volunteering in the parish often ask how to encourage involvement among teenagers. Most Sunday mornings, the teenagers are sitting with their families or, in some cases, actively participating in liturgy. There is excitement and possibility wrapped around engaging teenagers with social media and empowering them to use it.

A 15-year-old teenager I know uses Twitter daily to express her thoughts about her day or relationships. She likes that it gives her an outlet to share her thoughts and photographs instantly. She enjoys the challenge of capturing a thought in one or two sentences. She is mildly irked when her thoughts bubble over the 140 characters in Twitter. Since she is already at ease typing out updates in her life via social media, I asked if she would be interested in using Twitter with her parish activities. She smiled right away.

She was already engaging her friends on Twitter when it came to Sunday evening reminders for meetings. She was where they were and vice versa. It was a fun place for them to be themselves. Given that she and her peers would scan Twitter daily, she said it was helpful for some of those in her youth group to receive reminders from her via Twitter.

When using social media with teenagers and young adults, encourage them to think creatively when processing an experience. There are times that adults will motivate teenagers to be creative with a process which leads to teenagers accepting the responsibility and challenge of a project. Once the project takes off, the adults might take back ownership of the project, sometimes putting a crimp in creativity. It becomes important for adults to realize that given the nature of social media, the younger generation will have a better grasp of how to use the various sites. However, it is important to note that adults should still keep an eye on projects to make sure that whatever final project gets shared on social media is still under the auspices of the parish. There is often a fine line between guidance and hampering creativity.

# CHAPTER 4

# Putting Social Media to Work in Your Parish

**THINK ABOUT ALL THE WONDERFUL THINGS GOING ON IN YOUR PARISH.** How is genuine community being created? What new things are being tried that could be shared with other parishioners? How are parishioners able to learn from each other? How, then, might you put social networking to use in order to share all this good news with others? It is one thing to read a blurb in a Sunday bulletin; social media takes sharing such information to a whole new dimension by adding photographs and stories in real time.

Starting new endeavors and projects is uncomfortable

for many of us. There are already enough tasks to manage without adding more. While social media might be seen as one more thing to do, the value it holds for enhancing our ministerial efforts is well worth the time and energy. Let's look at practical steps for putting it to work.

## Selling social media to leaders and others

One of the challenges of initiating social media as part of parish ministry is convincing those around us to adopt a new mind-set. This is true of new projects or ideas in most organizations. Change is often met with heavy resistance. The conversation keeps moving but the project or initiative itself stops.

■ *It's best to be flexible when beginning the conversation around social media.* Break the ice by inviting several members to join a social networking committee. These should be people who have a genuine concern for the life of the parish as well as an interest in learning to use technology. Since the latter can be done in a reasonable amount of time, it is not necessary to recruit experts or to be weighed down by the lack of technological savvy. Set deadlines, but remain open to each person's individual learning curve.

■ *Parishes that are just beginning this initiative will want to try one social network at a time.* For example, if your parish has a website but no other presence online, you might want to pick one ministry to try out on a single site, such as Pinterest for catechists, or Twitter for liturgical ministers. If your parish currently has a Facebook page, think about one or two other ways to integrate it into the parish. Go another route by encouraging one or two ministries to try Flickr for photograph storage, or to use LinkedIn to connect with other parishes in the diocese.

■ *Patience, as well as openness to feedback from parishioners, is important.* Be willing to have a conversation about change with staff members, committee heads, and volunteers. Chances are that you are just as invested in your specific ministry as anyone else is in theirs, so opening up a dialog is essential. Keep an open heart and mind to what may come of social networking for your ministry and parish.

■ *Once initial ideas surface, questions will arise around finances.* Will it require extra equipment? Additional staff? Specialized training? The good news is that social media has been created in such a way that it can be done with basic technology. Chances are the basic tools are already in place. In many cases the only equipment needed is a computer and a digital camera, or even a smart phone with a built-in camera. Access to the internet is an obvious necessity, but that is almost a given in today's technological world.

## Taking the first steps

Another challenge is getting parishioners to understand that building social media into our ministries takes time. Like any other new project, building the pieces in small increments is essential. Small success stories will eventually lead to larger ones. Here are some steps to get the process started.

- *Recruit volunteers.* These are people who are willing to set time aside weekly or bi-weekly to maintain a site. Social media sites work best when they are continually updated so that information remains relevant. A parish might address this need by dividing work into two-month assignments among staff members or volunteers. Each person might then take responsibility for being the sole updater. Another option is assembling a team of volunteers to assume responsibility for one or more sites.

Recruiting volunteers might begin with announcements from the pulpit and in the parish bulletin or newsletter. A better option is through direct invitation. Parish leaders might consider inviting one or two people from particular ministries to participate. In religious education programs, for example, responsibilities for posting messages and photos might be divided among a couple of catechists at the beginning of the year, with other catechists or parents picking up the task for each month of the program. Teenagers might take pictures at parish events and then update the Flickr or the Picasa page. One or two young adults might assist ministerial groups, such as social ministry coordinators, DREs, and the pastoral council, in creating the basic pages. They might be considered unofficial technology consultants. You might also approach persons who have recently retired and are currently enrolled in computer and technology classes. Be open to including various age groups as volunteer recruitment begins and then expands.

■ *Set up online sites.* Key to the process is getting a social media presence, such as on Facebook, Pinterest, or Flickr, up and running. Begin by organizing a committee of representatives from several groups—such as youth ministry, liturgical ministry, outreach, pastoral council, and religious education—in order to evaluate social networking. Don't forget the pastor. Even if he is not fully involved in the initiative, keep him abreast of the progress of the initiative.

■ *Get started.* Once the group is assembled, identify a few projects or activities that lend themselves to a social media approach and that will, as a result, generate renewed interest among parishioners. For example, use Facebook and Twitter to publicize dates, times, and registration information for parish events, like a ministry fair or outreach project. Start a Pinterest site for families in the religious education program, and invite two parents from each grade level to update it each week. One pin might have themes and images of what the fourth graders are doing, and then, the following week, pictures of first graders could be added. Initiate a closed Facebook or LinkedIn group for adults who are interested in a

Scripture series or in faith-sharing groups. Each week the leaders can ask one of the members to post a short reflection on the site as a way of generating conversation.

*Here are some other "quick start" ideas:*

- Use Flickr to generate involvement in a Thanksgiving food drive. Post photos of volunteers who distribute food to clients in a diocesan or parish soup kitchen.

- Launch a Twitter site for liturgical ministries. Invite lectors to take turns tweeting reflections or a spiritual insight from the Sunday readings. Broaden the effort by including eucharistic ministers, choir members, and greeters.

- Start a Tumblr account for teenagers who are preparing for a service project. Post videos and blogs that tell what the youth will be doing, and how the parish can offer support and encouragement.

- Upload homilies as podcasts as a way to allow traveling parishioners to stay in touch with Sunday worship.

- Generate interest throughout the parish by launching a new site in conjunction with liturgical seasons, such as Advent or Lent. Use photos, images, stories, and reflections that are keyed to the seasonal themes.

## Keeping social media work manageable

The variety of social media makes it easy to spread the work around so it can be split among various groups. Once a committee is up and running, it can start to create a network of volunteers to manage and contribute to various sites. For example, a Flickr or Tumblr site can be kept current by inviting various groups—such as liturgical environment, children's choir, and senior care ministry—to be responsible for posting photos for a week out of the year. Perhaps someone from the facilities and grounds committee can take pictures of the parish hall, worship space, and gathering areas during the different liturgical and natural seasons.

After the photos are taken, individuals can upload them at the end of the week or even by the next day. The immediacy of posts keeps users interested in what is going on around them. If one parish group becomes the social media liaison for one week or month of the year, this spreads out the work and shares specific activities at the same time. This responsible group would make sure items are posted on a timely basis and that photographs are relatively new. This approach does not depend upon one person to do all the updates, but upon a community that shows its pride in the work they do.

Before deciding what might be best for your ministry or your parish, think about what you want to accomplish by adding social media to what you are already doing on a daily and weekly basis. Jumping into too many sites at once is overwhelming. Opt, instead, to experiment with a site like Pinterest during the academic year, and

Facebook during the summer, to get a feel for what each offers and to link with seasonal events and programs. Play with different social media sites until you find one or two that might really fit your parish and ministries.

### Parish versus personalized sites

Besides using social media to establish a parish presence online, many parish leaders use personalized accounts to talk about their ministry. Let's use a fictional scenario to describe what this means. Father Peter at St. Mary's Parish creates his own Twitter account to tweet about the ministries and news at his parish. He might use the profile name: SMFPeter. The expectation would be that, when looking up SMFPeter online, one would find information about the parish but "personalized" by Father Peter.

Since so many people in the parish are likely to be using some kind of social media, it is an easy step to ask them to "like" or "follow" the parish site through their personal Facebook, Twitter, or other accounts. Doing so increases visibility and allows the parish presence to multiply without much effort on the part of parish leaders.

## NEXT...

▶ While social media will never replace the community created and sustained through worship and direct ministry, it does have the potential to ramp up efforts at evangelization and fellowship. But there can be pitfalls. We'll look at some of them in the next chapter.

## THOUGHTS TO PONDER...

- *Think about a few people in your parish who are social media users and who might be looking for a new ministry or who might be invigorated with the possibility of trying something new. How do you invite them to take part in something that will help the life of your parish or specific ministry?*

- *What is the biggest hurdle for you and your parish using social media?*

- *What are some things you hope to gain personally or professionally from using social media?*

## 100% chance of miracle

A priest I know uses his Twitter account to invite people to Mass at the Catholic Center where he is the chaplain. His tweets are sometimes a little goofy but always engaging, including his recent post about the 9 PM. Mass frequented by undergraduates: "3.5 hours to Mass. Starting lineup: presider, Fr. John; deity, God. Expected attendance: 300 students. Altar conditions: sacred. Be there!"

# CHAPTER 5

# Pitfalls and Possibilities

**STARTING A NEW ENDEAVOR BRINGS BOTH EXCITE-MENT OVER POSSIBILITIES AND ANXIETY OVER PO-TENTIAL PITFALLS.** This is especially true when embarking into the field of social media. Here are a few things to watch for as you begin this venture.

### Stay enthusiastic in the face of skepticism

In Chapter 3, we looked at ways to sell social media to others in your parish. There are bound to be skeptics when it comes to venturing so far afield from traditional methods of communication and conversation. Some might turn down your ideas for using social media for ministry and evangelization. The best option is to go slow and to keep track of any positive responses you receive from the efforts you are making.

Even if everyone is on board with the idea, it is still a good idea to go slow in the beginning. Putting too many ideas to work at the same time will not be helpful. The different social media sites were created to build upon each other and various platforms. It's a bit like learning to play a sport like basketball. At first you become comfortable with just getting onto the court and dribbling the ball. Once you master this, you start to move up and down on the basketball court. Now you and the other players can learn from each other and, in the process, discover each other's strengths. Together you create a team that complements and motivates each other. It is the same thing with social media. Get out there and try something, knowing you will grow with it.

### Be mindful of minors

Many organizations, such as the National Federation for Catholic Youth Ministry, have specific guidelines on how to communicate with young people through social networking. Many of these advise against parish volunteers becoming friends with minors on their personal social media sites. It's much safer for all concerned to create a closed group through the parish that is monitored by those in leadership and accessible to parents. Check with your diocesan office for specific guidelines when it comes to using social media for youth ministry and other online activity.

Because young people are so adept at using social

networking, they are often eager to volunteer for parish initiatives involving this form of communication. Here are some words of caution about involving teens in your social media efforts as well as other issues having to do with minors:

- When creating any account on social media that involves adolescents, make sure it is overseen by at least two adults who have access to the account at all times.

- Remind young people who are posting items for the parish that they are representing the church. Respect must be maintained in all dialogs, along with professionalism throughout their posts.

- Obtain parental permission to use photographs of their children. Many organizations use just a first name when identifying people in photos. A table in the back of this book includes various websites with comprehensive social media policies that you can refer to.

- Be aware of not putting too much responsibility on the teenagers and young adults of the parish. If social networking is something adopted by the greater parish, then it is imperative that parishioners of all ages get involved in some capacity to showcase the breadth of ministries.

## Watch where you click

There is no question that abuse of social media is a problem. Digging up information on an old friend or an acquaintance has been termed by some as "Facebook stalking" and is an unhealthy use of social media. It is best to draw a line between the kind of personal relationships that can be maintained through online sites, and those that should remain strictly within the realm of ministerial service and professional behavior. It is important to retain boundaries that respect individuals' privacy.

While it is certainly possible to use a personal account for ministerial purposes, it is important to maintain a balance between the two uses. If the aim is to promote and encourage faith among those in the parish, create an account that helps you do that. This might best be done with an account like SMFPeter (see Chapter 4). Or, to use another example, perhaps "Catechist Kate" helps a catechist engage with students and families. This personalizes social media as well as links it to specific ministries and purposes. If you want to enter social media for yourself, make sure your reasons don't include expecting those for whom you work to become your fans or followers.

## THOUGHTS TO PONDER...

- *What questions remain about using social media in your parish? How can you find answers that will help you move forward in creative ways?*

- *How do you see yourself as being an example of Jesus Christ through social media?*

# The possibilities of social media

During World Communications Day in 2011, Pope Benedict XVI used the account of the Journey to Emmaus (Luke 24:13-35) to make a point about social media's potential within the church. This story shows us two individuals who are journeying after the resurrection. Along their walk, Jesus joins them without them being able to recognize him. They share stories with each other and listen as the man—who is later revealed to them in the Eucharist as the risen Christ—walks them through the Scriptures beginning with Moses. We hear in the gospel that toward the end of the journey, the pair asks Jesus to stay with them, and that he took bread, said the blessing, broke it, and gave it to them. It was through the Eucharist they were able to fully see Christ in front of them. Christ led them to that moment through his appearance and conversation.

In the Emmaus journey, said the pope, we learn that we can draw people forth if we have the patience and ability to listen to their deepest desires. Through our sustained relationships that are face-to-face and in social media, we have the ability to help each other get to a more genuine place in our lives of faith. It moves forward from just meeting someone at a social outing or working on a social justice project together to now sharing the Eucharist with one another on Sundays. Social media has that ability to move us from point A to point B without breaking our stride. Pope Benedict XVI spoke about people already revealing themselves to each other but noted that we must do so in authentic ways.

Within the context of our parish, we realize that being authentic means continued participation in the life of our parish as well as being open to deepening our faith lives with one another. This foundational knowledge of a deeper desire to seek the risen Christ in our social media interactions enables us to build our parish in ways that move beyond traditional measures. The Emmaus story shows us that without Jesus' retelling of the Scripture and sharing the Eucharist, it could have been just a story of three people meeting on the street. Intentionality, paired with a desire to listen and engage, elevates that encounter in a meaningful way.

Like Pope Benedict, we have good reason to be excited. Social media has the ability to generate excitement within the community no matter what our age. And that excitement can permeate into the pews and through the community, sending a message that embracing this media is embracing the future.

# Appendix

## GUIDELINE SOURCES

The following table includes organizations that have established guidelines for social media, technology and electronics.

| ORGANIZATION | EXPLANATION |
|---|---|
| **USCCB** – United States Conference of Catholic Bishops | An in-depth explanation of social media and how it can be used within a parish |
| http://www.usccb.org/about/communications/social-media-guidelines.cfm#guidelines | |
| **NFCYM** – National Federation of Catholic Youth Ministry | Outlines how to communicate with children and teenagers via social media |
| http://www.nfcym.org/resources/technology/guidelines.htm | |
| **Archdiocese of Milwaukee** | Good idea how to create a policy within a diocese |
| http://www.archmil.org/offices/safeguarding/Social-Networking-Policy.htm | |
| **Diocese of Dallas** | Comprehensive social media plan |
| http://www.cathdal.org/files/SocialMediaPolicy.pdf | |

# Facebook | facebook.com

**PRIMARY USE**: Networking and information sharing for individuals who set up profiles with personal information and some work history

Networking for businesses or corporations who set up a fan page or business page

| SECONDARY USE | SUGGESTED IDEAS | INTEGRATION |
|---|---|---|
| • Photo sharing<br><br>• News sharing<br><br>• Staying in touch with former classmates and old friends<br><br>• Following news for a company or organization<br><br>• Playing games online<br><br>• Individual messages and e-mails can also be sent through this site | • Announcing parish events<br><br>• Posting photos from parish events<br><br>• Sharing news and information<br><br>• Posting links to Sunday readings<br><br>• Posting parish videos<br><br>• Create closed Facebook groups for faith-sharing opportunities via social media | • A parish can decide to have one Facebook page for its parishioners<br><br>• A parish can also decide to have several Facebook pages: one for the parish and a few for specific ministries<br><br>• Searching for a church that has a Facebook page and parish website will help answer questions for those who are new or visiting a parish |

# Twitter | twitter.com

**PRIMARY USE**: Information sharing in 140 characters or less which are called tweets

Ability to follow an organization or individual to receive targeted information

| SECONDARY USE | SUGGESTED IDEAS | INTEGRATION |
| --- | --- | --- |
| • Sharing news and photographs | • Sending out news or reminders about parish events<br><br>• Links to posted photographs<br><br>• Tweeting of gospel message in 140 characters or less<br><br>• Giving a thought for the day | • Create a Twitter feed to help send out timely reminders and announcements<br><br>• Put your Twitter feed on your parish website to inform people of news and events<br><br>• Adding a Twitter feed to your website to share Mass times for Holy Days of Obligation |

# LinkedIn | linkedin.com

**PRIMARY USE**: Professional networking site that allows people and businesses to connect easily

| SECONDARY USE | SUGGESTED IDEAS | INTEGRATION |
|---|---|---|
| • Share business and work-related information<br><br>• Connect to potential employees and employers<br><br>• Seek recommendations from previous employers or co-workers | • Creating a group specific for your parishioners<br><br>• Creating a group for area churches who are using social media<br><br>• Using this as a place to find support for fundraising opportunities | • Use this as a way to connect to specific parish groups in your city and diocese<br><br>• Create a group for job seekers in the parish as a way to network and share job search tips |

# Google+ (Google Plus) | google.com

**PRIMARY USE:** Networking site that allows for video chats and conferencing

| SECONDARY USE | SUGGESTED IDEAS | INTEGRATION |
|---|---|---|
| • Sharing news and photographs<br><br>• Posting videos<br><br>• Video conferencing<br><br>• Recommendations from previous employers or co-workers | • Creating specific circles for religious education teachers, soup kitchen volunteers<br><br>• Video chat<br><br>• Using Google-specific applications such as Google Drive that help you keep track of phone numbers and liturgical ministry schedules | • Creating Google circles for groups post-retreat to keep in touch with each other<br><br>• Create an invitation to have an informal conversation on Google Hangouts for those exploring the faith |

# Pinterest | pinterest.com

**PRIMARY USE**: Users can digitally keep track of items like they were pinning items to a corkboard in their kitchen

The actual act of pinning is the equivalent of copying and saving the web link to a specific page. And users can easily go back to specific subject pages to find items they are seeking

| SECONDARY USE | SUGGESTED IDEAS | INTEGRATION |
|---|---|---|
| • Sharing inspirational photographs and quotes<br><br>• View and store favorite recipes | • Creating specific boards for religious education classroom projects<br><br>• Themed boards for Advent or Lent that include photographs and special prayers<br><br>• Create a parish board for parishioners to pin and save their favorite recipes | • Share your Pinterest posts from a religious education class onto a Facebook page for your parish to let people know what classes are covering<br><br>• Create a specific link to your website onto Pinterest for your parish prayer |

# Tumblr | Tumblr.com

**PRIMARY USE:** Microblogging site that allows users to instantly share videos, quotes, links, photographs

Ability to capture and post videos directly with an iPhone or an Android

| SECONDARY USE | SUGGESTED IDEAS | INTEGRATION |
|---|---|---|
| • Instant publishing site that captures and shares various types of media<br><br>• Share or stream videos using Tumblr | • Creating a specific Tumblr site as the youth minister in your parish to try and integrate new media and social networking easily<br><br>• Integrating CYO or sports leagues teams with Tumblr to keep up with team updates, schedules, and photos | • Linking and sharing specific videos from YouTube through Tumblr |

# YouTube | YouTube.com

**PRIMARY USE**: Video sharing

| SUGGESTED IDEAS | INTEGRATION |
|---|---|
| • Sharing video clips from a parish event<br><br>• Promoting the parish through video<br><br>• Create a specific parish video channel where you can watch videos specific to one parish or a group of parishes<br><br>• Showcasing music specific to a parish choir<br><br>• Sharing audio for new music | • Tumblr account<br><br>• Share specific video links with new parishioners in a welcome e-mail<br><br>• Post or showcase one video on a parish website |

# **Flickr** | Flickr.com  **Picasa** | Picasa.com

**PRIMARY USE**: Photo sharing

| SUGGESTED IDEAS | INTEGRATION |
|---|---|
| • Sharing photographs in a timely way<br><br>• Show a range of events through photo albums<br><br>• Enabling many people to upload photos to a parish account<br><br>• Sharing audio for new music | • Put a link onto your parish website after you upload photos from a parish project or special event<br><br>• Link to photos and photo albums on a Facebook page |

# **Podcasts**

**PRIMARY USE**: Audio sharing

| SUGGESTED IDEAS | INTEGRATION |
|---|---|
| • Sharing homilies easily<br><br>• Recording talks from parish mission | • Post audio links to Facebook or Tumblr pages<br><br>• Create podcast page to save homilies and talks for parishioners who are homebound |